LEAVING THE
COMFORT ZONE

LEAVING THE COMFORT ZONE

A Call to Radical Christianity

Terry Crist

Leaving the Comfort Zone
Terry Crist
P. O. Box 35889
Tulsa, OK 74153

Copyright © 1991 by Terry Crist
Printed in the United States of America
ISBN: 0-88368-221-4

Unless otherwise indicated, all Scripture quotations are taken from
the *King James Version* of the Bible.

Contents

1

Awakening in the Slumber Zone

As the sun rapidly sinks into the horizon of the twentieth century, we are confronted with an overwhelming need of a Church of power.

We are living in a generation that is convulsed in sin. This is a generation of academic excellence, an age of unmatched technical skill, an era of unsurpassed technological development. Yet sadly we are also engulfed in moral retrogression, secular humanism, financial upheaval, and political instability.

There is mounting violence on every hand, and that without restriction to any country, city, race, or age category. No one is immune to this global assault. Crime is rapidly increasing throughout the world and ravaging the face of modern society. Like most nations on earth, the United States of America is engaged in a losing war against drugs and crime.

We are no longer shocked and outraged to hear of the most heinous of crimes occurring in our very own neighborhoods. Just a short while ago I awoke in the small hours of the night to the sound of sirens. A few blocks down the street from my house, a man was shot in the face and killed during an argument with his wife.

Yes indeed, **There is a generation, whose teeth are as swords, and their jaw teeth as knives...** (Prov. 30:14) — and today you and I are living in the very midst of that "faithless and perverse generation"! (Matt. 17:17.)

This Untoward Generation

Peter, the apostle, gave the warning when he cried out, **...Save yourselves from this untoward generation** (Acts 2:40). The word *untoward* has a number of meanings, but the one that would best fit this generation is "unfortunate."

Ours is an unfortunate generation. Famines rampage and decimate nations. Wars and revolutions deprive millions of their jobs, homes and families. Pollution blights the landscape. Malnutrition percentages soar in some places, while in others people have far too much. Even in seemingly prosperous nations like the United States, old folks still huddle in their homes in winter where they die of hypothermia, while the younger, stronger and healthier lounge in comfort with no thought for those less fortunate than they. Young and old alike book flights after having saved for months, to go and visit loved ones thousands of miles away. As they sit back peacefully dreaming about the joyful reunion ahead, the aircraft is suddenly hijacked or bombed by terrorist fanatics.

Truly this is an unfortunate generation. Something must be done to set it free from fear and destruction. There must come forth from the pulpits and pews around the globe a cry to people everywhere to save themselves from this untoward generation.

A Call to Arms

In the midst of this sin-ravaged generation, suddenly a clarion call has come from heaven, a command to arise, take in hand the sword of truth, and enter the good fight of faith.

This is not the hour for slumbering Christians to sit passively by and expect some outside intervention to miraculously rescue the twenty-first century. The responsibility for last days revival rests squarely upon our shoulders.

The only way the Church will ever arise in power is to first kneel in prayer.

While many wait and watch for a sovereign outside intervention, they ignore heaven's challenge to arise and push back the powers of the night. (Eph. 5:1-16.) Some time ago the Holy Spirit spoke to me and said, *"Until you confront what is, you will never experience what can be."* I believe that is true for the entire Body of Christ.

It is time that we begin to realize that the Church has not just been set in the earth to occupy space. We are not here to sit on comfortable pews, listen to motivating sermons and do nothing to affect the nature and destiny of our world. We are not here to gain a natural reputation for ourselves or to impress the world with our sanctity or prosperity. We are here to make an impact upon society through the power of the Gospel and to bring about a change in the hearts of men.

There is a vast difference between impressing society and making an impact upon it. Impressions are easily forgotten, while impacts leave lasting results.

People of Destiny

We in the Church must realize that we are aliens on a mission. God has set us here for a divine purpose, and that purpose must be fulfilled through the life of every believer.

God has a planned destiny for the life of each one of us, as well as for the Church as a corporate body. The Church has been in the mind of God since the foundation of the world was laid. (Eph. 3:11.) The Church is not an "after thought." It is not the result of some hastily conceived backup plan that was put into effect 2,000 years ago to save God from embarrassment because His primary plan had failed. God has always had an eternal destiny in mind for the Church as a whole and also for each of our individual lives.

Very few believers have a true sense of destiny for their lives. Most spend their entire existence in a state of perpetual wonderment. They pass their whole lives wondering what their purpose is or what is their calling in the Kingdom of God. As a pastor, I see far too many Christians who are wandering aimlessly through life with no purpose or direction. They lack fire and zeal.

Oh yes, they are "bound for heaven," because they have been born again. Their difficulty is not in preparing for heaven, it is in dealing with this earth. They are perpetually in a tranquil state of mediocre existence. Few believers ever dare to step past the line of mediocrity and "press toward the mark for the prize of their high calling in Christ Jesus." (Phil. 3:14.)

Once you catch a glimpse of your destiny in God, your life will never be the same. A vision of destiny will change every aspect of your life. It will alter the way you walk, talk, live and breathe. You will become a person of destiny.

People of destiny carry about them a purposeful air. They walk and talk boldly. They are confident, forceful men and women. They know and understand their mission in life. They have purposed in their hearts to make the necessary sacrifices and to accept the essential responsibilities of bringing about God's plan. People of destiny refuse to settle for anything less than God's perfect will in their lives.

Such people know that they are not living in this day and hour as a result of coincidence, but that God has strategically placed them in this particular time and place. Isaiah 41:4 declares that God is the One Who calls the generations from the beginning. That means that He orchestrates the generations. In the beginning of time, He determined to place *you* in this particular generation to serve as an end-time saint and minister.

People of destiny cannot be sidetracked. They may sometimes be enticed with false promises, but they will never allow that enticement to become a substitute for their divine purpose in life. If they happen to get off track, they are quick to repent, make the necessary adjustments and get back on course.

When a vision of destiny comes alive within you, you will not be content with anything less than the fulfillment of that vision. Material things will not fulfill you. Houses, automobiles, properties and bank accounts will not satisfy your deepest longings. Nothing will fill the void within except walking in the steps that God has chartered for your life.

Divine Unrest

Wherefore he saith, Awake thou that sleepest, and arise from the dead, and Christ shall give thee light.
Ephesians 5:14

I believe that a holy unrest is coming to the Church of North America. For too long we have been content with little victories and meager spoils. Now we must awake from our sleep, stir ourselves from our lethargy, and step forth into the glorious light of God's presence and power. There is much to be done in the crucial days that lie ahead.

Over the last few years I have begun to sense a feeling of divine unrest in the Church due to the apparent lack of spiritual productivity. I believe the Holy Spirit is now stripping away the deceptive facade of our fleshly strivings for achievement and revealing our true lack.

Comfortable people do not move. It's only when a divine discomfort comes that we are willing to examine where we actually are and whether or not we are truly being productive.

11

When I refer to spiritual productivity, I am not referring to charting out five-year plans or recording personal achievement objectives on our daily planners. I, along with many others, desire that which *really* produces quality and eternal fruit. What is needed by our wounded and hurting world is not the temporary salve of new resolutions and good intentions, but the true healing balm of Gilead which takes away the reproach of the nations.

Wake and Watch

And that, knowing the time, that now it is high time to awake out of sleep: for now is our salvation nearer than when we believed.

Romans 13:11

Awake, arise, engage the enemy — the battleground is revealed. Some are asleep while others hide in fear. What is your response to the blowing of the trumpet?

Therefore let us not sleep, as do others; but let us watch and be sober.

For they that sleep sleep in the night; and they that be drunken are drunken in the night.

But let us, who are of the day, be sober....

1 Thessalonians 5:6-8

As we progress through this book, I challenge you to awake from your sleep and watch soberly — to examine the confrontational nature of true Christ-like living.

2

Leaving the Comfort Zone

When Jesus came to this earth declaring the Gospel of the Kingdom, He violently shook up the religious order of the day. Instead of revealing Himself as a wise old theologian, He appeared on the scene as a young radical revolutionary with a whip in His hand and the fire of heaven in His eyes.

There was nothing subtle about the earthly ministry of the Lord Jesus Christ. Everything He did screamed of controversy. In fact, most of the time He seemed to go out of His way to engage the religious leaders of that day in direct confrontation. His goal in life was not to be offensive, but it was to reveal the heart of man.

While He healed their sick, raised their dead, cleansed their lepers, and cast out their demons, the zealous Pharisees continued to go to the synagogue every Sabbath day and pray — devoutly expressing their deepest longings for the coming of the Messiah.

Time and again, before their very eyes, our Lord literally fulfilled their prophetic Scriptures regarding His coming, yet they chose to ignore His obvious presence. Why? Because He did not fulfill their natural fleshy expectations of what the long-awaited Messiah would be like. This man overthrew no natural governments and set up no immediate physical kingdom; therefore, He could not be the Promised One.

False Image of the Christ

One of the reasons why the twentieth-century Church has not been conformed to the image of Christ is because

13

we too have false expectations of what the Messiah is like. We must come to a proper understanding of Who He truly is or we will never experience what He desires to do within us.

We have all been called to be conformed to the image of Christ, but as long as we harbor false images of Him we will never be like Him. Instead, we will continually be conformed to the false image of what we mistakenly perceive Him to be.

I believe that for the past 1900 years much of the Church has been attempting to conform to a false image. Yet we wonder why we experience so little productivity in the Kingdom of God. We must see our Lord as He truly is, if we are ever to be changed into His likeness.

Far too many Christians have a mental image of our Lord as a sort of sixties flower child. They perceive Him as a "holdover hippie" who never made the transition into the seventies, let alone the eighties or nineties. They picture Him with long shoulder-length hair and a straggly beard, wearing a flowing white robe and leather sandals. Around His neck hangs a peace medallion, while His head is encircled with a soft blue halo. Behind His ear dangles a lone daisy as He skips gently through the tulips murmuring softly, "Peace, peace, peace."

As strange as it may seem, our Lord is envisioned by many as an effeminate philosopher who spent all of His time communing with nature, petting furry animals and chatting with small children — never raising His voice or experiencing any of the trials or tribulations associated with this life.

Such people forget that Jesus totally dispelled that image when He told His disciples, **Think not that I am come to send peace on earth: I came not to send peace, but a sword** (Matt. 10:34).

14

We expect the Messiah to look, dress and act a certain way today. In this respect, we are not unlike the religious order of Jesus' day. Just as He failed to live up to their fleshly expectations, so He will fail to live up to ours also.

Jesus was not an effeminate weakling, He was a powerful warrior. As God manifest in the flesh, He displayed the same warring nature the Old Testament Lord of Hosts possessed:

> **The Lord is a man of war: the Lord is his name.**
>
> **Exodus 15:3**

> **Lift up your heads, O ye gates; and be ye lift up, ye everlasting doors; and the King of glory shall come in.**
>
> **Who is this King of glory? The Lord strong and mighty, the Lord mighty in battle.**
>
> **Psalm 24:7,8**

Jesus Invaded the Earth

> **...For this purpose the Son of God was manifested, that he might destroy the works of the devil.**
>
> **1 John 3:8**

The Amplified Bible version of this verse states, **...The reason the Son of God was made manifest (visible) was to undo (destroy, loosen and dissolve) the works the devil [has done].**

I want you to understand that Jesus Christ came into the earth for one reason, and that was to dethrone Satan, god of this world.

God sent His Son into the earth with one objective in mind — to undo, loosen, and dissolve every work that the devil has done. Jesus was sent with a divine commission — to annihilate completely the power of the enemy.

When Jesus operated in the power of the anointing, He was constantly undoing, loosening and dissolving the effects that sin and darkness had brought into the world.

The bondage of sickness, disease and torment was destroyed because of the anointing that was upon Him.

In everything that He said and did, Jesus was aggressively attacking the powers of darkness. When He healed the sick, cast out demons, preached the Gospel or made intercession for the people, He was engaged in spiritual warfare. When He confronted the pious, self-righteous Pharisees in their powerless traditions and outright sin, He was challenging Satan himself. Unafraid of the consequences of suffering and death, His mission in life was completely consuming.

Jesus in the Combat Zone

For the first time, at the young age of twelve years, Jesus stepped out of His comfort zone. His earthly parents had taken Him with them to Jerusalem for a time of special worship. Thinking He was with friends or family members, they departed without Him — only to discover to their dismay that He was nowhere to be found. After three days of searching for Him, His parents located Him in the temple where He was asking questions of the doctors of the law. When asked why He had remained behind in Jerusalem, He replied, **...I must be about my Father's business...**(Luke 2:49).

Jesus knew that in order to be obedient to the high calling of God, He had to leave behind every comfort zone. That's why He could address His followers with such authority and boldly declare, **If any man come to me, and hate not his father, and mother, and wife, and children, and brethren, and sisters, yea, and his own life also, he cannot be my disciple** (Luke 14:26).

It was on the cross that this message was put to the test as Jesus in His agony looked on the pain-ridden face of His mother and turned her over to John, saying to her, **...Woman, behold thy son!** (John 19:26).

Jesus' Challenge to Discipleship

Radical Christianity simply means forsaking all and cleaving to Christ alone. It is precisely such a step of self-denial to which Jesus calls each of those who wish to follow Him.

The Gospel narratives are loaded with various instances in which Jesus challenged people to leave behind, give up, and forsake everything in order to be used in the Kingdom of God. Our Lord knew that men and women could never do the perfect will of God as long as they sat in the safety of the comfort zone.

When the rich young ruler came to Jesus seeking eternal life, the Lord responded by challenging him to give up, forsake, and leave behind the one thing that was dearest to his flesh — his earthly riches. (Matt. 19:16-22.)

When a certain man came to Jesus pledging to follow Him after the death of his father, Jesus responded by telling the man to let the (spiritually) dead attend to such things, but for him to go immediately and begin to preach the Gospel. (Luke 9:57-60.)

In the same passage, another man was commanded to depart for the mission field without even bidding farewell to his family. (Luke 9:61,62.)

When Jesus called the twelve disciples into the work of the ministry, He challenged them to give up the thing dearest to each of them. If you and I can fully understand the disciples' call to ministry, we will better be able to understand our own.

The call to the disciples was a divine decree, not a sweet suggestion. Jesus didn't even give them an option when He called them into the work of the Kingdom. He simply passed by and said, "Follow Me." (Matt. 4:19-22, 9:9; John 1:43.) He didn't encourage them with promises of profit-sharing, stock options, retirement plans, fringe benefits or other such "perks." They were not enticed with the prospects of filling important positions on the "governing board" of the "new church" Jesus was forming. The comfort zone was never considered. The cost of discipleship was.

God doesn't really care whether or not you and I are comfortable. His primary concern is whether or not we are obedient! If obedience and comfort can be followed down the same road, so be it. But if we ever come to a fork in the road and obedience leads one way while comfort leads another, we must forsake comfort and choose the path of obedience.

Far too many promising ministers have never achieved their high calling in God because they have been afraid to move out of the comfort zone. Fear paralyzes the administration of the perfect will of God in their lives, preventing them from living on the cutting edge of radical Christianity. This fear is an evil spirit that must be resisted with great force. (2 Tim. 1:6,7.) It cannot be passively ignored. *Fear causes spiritual paralysis.* Until it is confronted, you will never experience the freedom to obey God.

Many times the comfort zone has such great attraction because that is where family and friends dwell. Negative peer pressure thrives in the comfort zone, subtly eroding away at the pioneering spirit that God has placed in every born-again believer. It is a killer of destinies.

Another deceptive danger that dwells in the comfort zone is mediocrity. This subtle enemy manifests itself through phrases such as, "Relax, don't strive so hard," "Be like the rest of us," "Just be content with the way things are." Suddenly the status quo, rather than the perfect will of God, becomes the measuring stick for life. Mediocrity and a love of the status quo will always spell death to God's divine destiny for your life.

Leaving the Comfort Zone

Every man or woman who is truly called of God to an end-time ministry will, at one point or another, be required to leave the comfort zone in order to fulfill the will of the Lord.

The house of Terah represented Abram's comfort zone. (Gen. 11:26-31.) In Haran, where he had gone to live with his family, the word of the Lord came to Abram commanding him to arise and depart from the land of his father. He was instructed to set out on a spiritual journey, by faith, not knowing where he was headed. (Gen. 12:1; Heb. 11:8.)

The land of Canaan represented Joseph's comfort zone. (Gen. 37:1.) But in order to fulfill the ultimate plan of God for his life, he had to graduate from the status of a bragging boy to that of a man of wisdom and understanding. This evolutionary process could not be accomplished in the land of his father amidst the security of home and family. God allowed certain seemingly negative events to take place in Joseph's life, moving him away from his beloved Canaan and into far-off Egypt, thus divinely positioning him for the future salvation of his entire family. (Gen. 45:1-8.)

The winepress represented Gideon's comfort zone. (Judg. 6:11.) The word of the Lord came to him there declaring him to be a mighty man of valor. It was far easier for Gideon to remain in hiding in the winepress than it was to assume his God-ordained position as a brilliant military strategist in the land of Israel. (Judg. 6:13,14.)

The brook Cherith represented Elijah's comfort zone. (1 Kings 17:1-6.) After having been led by the Spirit of God to this place of miraculous provision, Elijah was forced to abandon his comfort zone. God had to dry up the brook in order to motivate Elijah to return to the forefront of prophetic ministry. (1 Kings 17:7-9.)

The warm fire represented Peter's comfort zone. (John 18:15-18.) The reality of Jesus' betrayal and arrest, and fear for his own life, drove Peter to seek the security of a safe, comfortable place on the sidelines where he could watch what transpired without having to be a party to it. It was there, as he basked in the warmth of the fire, that he was pressured into denying that he even knew the Messiah. Peter's downfall came about because, instead of meeting adversity with truth, he chose the false security of the comfort zone. (John 18:17-27.)

The feet of Gamaliel represented Paul's comfort zone. (Acts 22:3.) It was there that he was instructed in what he later termed "the perfect manner of the law." His future was molded as "an Hebrew of the Hebrews," and "a Pharisee, the son of a Pharisee." (Phil. 3:5; Acts 23:6.) There, at the feet of the leading Hebrew scholar of the day, his human reasoning was appeased, his superior intellect satiated. Sadly enough, later on he noted that, in the light of the knowledge of the Lord, he had come to consider all this great learning as mere "dung." (Phil. 3:5-8.)

Like so many of the great men and women of God, it is in times of comfort and ease that you and I will encounter the greatest opportunities to compromise. After many victories campaigning in the fields of battle, one season David decided to remain at home in the comfort zone while the kings went forth to battle. That was the year that he fell into sin with Bathsheba. (1 Chron. 20:1; 2 Sam. 11:1-5.)

The comfort zone provides a false sense of security. I have discovered that living in war-torn Lebanon in the will of God is far more secure than living in peaceful Tulsa, Oklahoma, out of the will of God. The greatest security that we can possibly know is to be found in the center of the perfect will of the Lord. There is no true security except in obedience to the divine directives of Almighty God.

I challenge you to come out of the comfort zone and live your life on the cutting edge. Once you experience radical Christianity, you will never again be content with mediocrity.

3

Breaking the Old Wineskin

**No man putteth a piece of new cloth into an old garment,
for that which is put in to fill it up taketh from the garment,
and the rent is made worse.**

Matthew 9:16

Here we see Jesus illustrating the principle of the tattered garment. Permit me to illustrate it for you in this way:

Most of us own at least one favorite old piece of clothing. Perhaps you have a beloved pair of worn-out blue jeans. They have been with you for ages and have become closer to you than your dearest friend. Through the years they have been conformed to your individual personality and physical form. (I have such a pair of cherished old jeans myself. I often joke that all I have to do when I get out of bed in the morning is whistle for them, and they respond instantly.)

The problem with comfortable old garments is that just about the time they're really broken in well, they have become worn out. If you take a new piece of material that has never been washed or pre-shrunk and use it as a patch on those old faded jeans, you are going to have future problems. There will come a time when the new patch will begin to shrink and pull away from the old cloth. Through time the new material will cause a worse tear than the one it was used to repair.

It doesn't make sense to put a new patch on an old worn-out garment. The best alternative is to throw away the old piece of clothing and buy a brand new one.

God has determined for the Church of His Son Jesus Christ to be purged from her filthy garments of self-righteousness in this hour. The garments of pride, ambition, self-will, self-sufficiency, self-promotion, and divisiveness will be purged in the last days. (Is. 4:4.)

Jesus purchased for Himself a bride free from filthy rags. He gave His life on the cross of Calvary, suffering and dying, shedding His precious blood, **that he might present it to himself a glorious church, not having spot, or wrinkle, or any such thing; but that it should be holy and without blemish** (Eph. 5:27).

New Wine in New Bottles

Neither do men put new wine into old bottles: else the bottles break, and the wine runneth out, and the bottles perish: but they put new wine into new bottles, and both are preserved.

Matthew 9:17

I believe that one of the most significant prophetic words that God is speaking to the Church of the nineties in that this is the hour of the breaking of the old wineskin. The things that we have used in the past to house the glory of God and to contain His authority must be removed in order to receive the new. The basic principle illustrated by Jesus in this verse from Matthew is:

The old must be abolished in order for the new to be established. (Heb. 10:9.)

As we study the principle of the wineskin, we will learn an eternal truth. In ancient times, a wineskin was created from animal products. A winemaker would take the internal organs or a portion of the cured hide of a goat or other animal and use it to create a wineskin.

Shortly afterwards, into the wineskin would be poured new wine. As the new wine began to ferment, it would expand and increase in volume. During the fermentation process, the supple wineskin would increase in elasticity along with the new wine. But after a period of time, the skin would be formed into a permanent shape and begin to harden.

After the wine had been drunk and the wineskin was empty, it was dangerous to refill it with new wine. As the new wine fermented and expanded, it would crack the hardened skin, causing it to burst and lose its valuable contents.

Many people are attempting to place the new move of God's Spirit in the same mold as previous visitations.

One day as I was meditating on this subject, the Holy Spirit said to me, "For many in My Church, sudden expansion would mean destruction."

At one time or another we have all asked, "Lord, why are we not experiencing the power of the Holy Spirit as You predestined for the end time?" I believe the reason is because God has self-contained the Church for a season while He is creating a new wineskin within us.

As I travel across North America, as well as in foreign countries, I repeatedly hear the cry of frustrated ministers who are desperate for new wine. That is all well and good, but first we must be thoroughly prepared to receive and contain that new wine.

I am going to make a statement here that may not bring you to your feet in excitement, yet it will set you free:

God is more interested in us as individuals than He is in our ministries.

God is more concerned about developing our personal character than about seeing signs, wonders and power gifts operating in our life. What manner of father would give his three-year-old child a .45-caliber automatic handgun and say, "Have a nice day at the target range"? Powerful weapons are reserved exclusively for mature individuals who have been instructed and trained in how to use them for maximum effect.

New Wineskin for Fresh Wine

I believe that one reason God has not released the full force of authority that is coming to the Church is because we are not yet in a position to handle it. We are asking for new wine, but God is saying to us, "First I must give you a new wineskin."

The wineskin is representative of the authority structure that God desires to give us.

Some time ago I stood on the platform of our church and observed the people. Suddenly I began to see them through the eyes of the Spirit. What I saw startled me. Instead of seeing one collective wineskin, I saw various types and sizes of individual wineskins. I saw Pentecostal wineskins, Word of Faith wineskins, denominational wineskins, and Catholic wineskins.

Up to now, our former wineskins have been acceptable. The structure has been adequate in the past. But it is time for fresh wine in this hour.

The old wineskin was sufficient for a season. It certainly contained the old wine. Now the old wineskin is beginning to dry out and become brittle. God desires to give us a new one. He seeks to reveal a new wineskin that can house the fullness of the glory which He is eager to begin pouring out upon His people.

It has often been said that Church history reveals that the greatest persecutors of every new visitation of God are those who were on the forefront of the previous one. This often happens because people refuse to yield their old wineskin and allow the Lord to bring forth a new one.

Most Christians arrive at a stopping point in their quest for further revelation. They become satisfied with the measure of wine they possess, or the particular "brand" they are accustomed to drinking.

I have literally heard believers argue over which "brand" of spiritual wine is best:

"I believe the Word of Faith wine is the best. After all, it helped me to obtain my healing and prosperity."

"No, I disagree. The Restoration wine is better; it has more balance to it."

"But I only drink Kingdom wine. It has provoked me to maturity as a part of the Body of Christ."

"You're all wrong. The traditional Pentecostal wine is still the best because it has properly aged."

"But I like denominational wine. It has security and tradition."

"Charismatic wine is the best. It's gentle, not too assertive."

And on and on it goes. Suddenly, divisive spirits have taken over while we have been arguing which "brand" of church, ministry, or spirituality is the "right" one.

Oftentimes we reject the gifts of God given to the Church because they don't conform to our preconceived notions of what they should be like. We refuse to accept God's ministers and spokesmen from other segments of the Body of Christ because they don't speak our language, dress as we do, use our mannerisms, or worship according to our teachings and practices. If we are to contain the new wine of God's Spirit, we must be open to receive that wine in whatever form the Spirit desires to pour it out upon us — and from whatever vessel He chooses to use. To house that new wine, we must have new wineskins — renewed minds and hearts which have not grown old, brittle, hardened and complacent.

I have often admonished the congregation of my church never to grow comfortable where the things of God are concerned. I encourage them to live fervently in the Kingdom of God.

"When you dance," I tell them, "leap as high as you can. When you pray, do so with all your might. When you weep, cry hard. When you repent, pour out your heart so that all of heaven and hell can hear you."

It is amazing how some of the very ones who have become most accustomed to hearing me say these things are the first to automatically tune me out. It doesn't matter how loudly I scream or how violently I wave my arms and pound upon the pulpit. I could turn up the sound system to ear-splitting decibels and still there would be some who would sleep right through the service.

You see, we are all in danger of becoming too accustomed to the moving of the Spirit. That is why the Lord is sending peculiar anointings into the Church in this hour. Because a peculiar anointing will get our attention, rouse us from our indolence and lethargy, and force us to wake up and give heed to the Word of the Lord.

4

How Radical Is Radical?

Most believers have not progressed very far beyond the initial revelation that they received in the new-birth experience. I challenge us to be completely honest about ourselves. How far have you and I progressed in spiritual maturity since we were baptized in the Holy Spirit?

Oh, we clap now in church. We raise our hands in praise and worship. We sing in tongues occasionally. And if the music is just right, you might even catch us dancing a little. We intercede in the spirit and every so often we actually cast out demons.

But when we encounter old friends from previous church groups or moves of God, what happens? We usually bow and compromise:

"Well, I really don't clap very loudly, raise my hands that often, or dance that much. I do speak in tongues, it's true, but only now and then, and only a few words at a time. I do intercede, but quietly and in private, and I only cast out small demons. After all, I'm not a radical."

Unconditional Obedience

How radical is radical? The best definition that I can give you of a "radical" is *one who obeys the perfect will of God for his or her life without fear, favor or regard to men.* Doing the works of Jesus without apology qualifies you for the cutting edge. Living on the cutting edge is nothing more spectacular than obeying your divine commission. The supernatural is not always spectacular. You can aspire to nothing higher than doing the will of the Father.

If God's high calling for your life is to be the church custodian, and you fulfill that commission with joy and obedience, then you are a radical.

If the perfect will of God for your life is to be a missionary to Africa, and you settle for the comfort and ease of doing anything else, then you are not a radical. Radical Christianity is not measured by great feats of religious activity, it is measured by simple obedience.

Most believers have not progressed very far spiritually. Many times it is because they are afraid of being labeled as "radical."

Frequently people call or write our offices desiring information on spiritual warfare or deliverance. And yet when they come visit our services and see that warfare and deliverance first hand, it is usually not quite what they had expected.

"It's too loud and unorthodox," they complain. I am amazed at how many people expect war to be nice, gentle and orderly. I have heard veterans of military conflicts describe war as something similar to a violent nightmare. It is oftentimes loud, frightening, confusing, and laborous.

Spiritual resistance is usually not encountered by simply preaching about spiritual warfare and deliverance. It is encountered when we begin to demonstrate these important truths. The devil will allow us to preach about certain subjects as long as we like, just as long as we don't actually begin to put them into practice.

The fear of being labeled "radical" has prevented many people from arising and assuming their rightful position in spiritual authority. The threat of controversy has caused them to draw back from present-day truth.

Here is another example of what I am talking about: We pray for God to raise up true prophets in the land. Yet when they begin to prophesy, often we attribute their prophecies to inside information or even the work of familiar spirits.

We pray for angels to be revealed to us. Yet when someone says, "I saw an angel today," we think, "Sure you did; and I saw Elvis at the supermarket!"

One morning we wake up and suddenly declare, "By faith I'm going to begin living according to biblical principles of finance." Then when we do and God begins to bless us by meeting our financial needs, we are quick to exclaim, "I can't *believe* it!"

Are you beginning to understand what I am saying? We really haven't progressed very far beyond our previous level of spirituality.

Another example: Many times we are spiritually moved in missionary services. Emotionally we determine to obey the will of God — as long as it doesn't involve the words "Africa" or "Asia"!

Most pastors will painfully identify with what I am about to say: Countless times I have heard individuals pledge their undying loyalty to the work of God in our local church. That loyalty is soon tested when the offering plate is passed. Then it quickly becomes apparent that their commitment was one of convenience, not sacrificial giving.

Growing up in a Pentecostal environment, I often viewed various individuals cry out in prayer for any hidden sin to be exposed and removed.

"Oh, God," they would fervently pray, "if there is any area of my life that is not pleasing to You, I want You to purge me."

Then when the purging process began, suddenly self-righteousness and self-justification would rear its ugly head and they would start making every excuse in the world for their wrong attitudes and actions.

"Lord," we pray so earnestly and devoutly, "we want a pastor, a true shepherd who is concerned for us."

Then when the pastor starts to shepherd the flock, he is quickly accused of trying to take control over it for his own benefit.

I realize that I am belaboring the point, but it is important for us to see ourselves as we really are. If we are to contain the new wine of God's Spirit, we must have a new wineskin in which to house it. Before we will ever be ready to receive the apostles and prophets of the twenty-first century, we must learn how to receive the evangelists, pastors, and teachers who are already moving among us.

Judge Not, But Receive the Spirit

God is beginning to reveal certain things in the earth, things which are unlike anything that we have ever witnessed before. These manifestations of God cannot be received or contained in an old wineskin.

The natural response to anything unfamiliar is rejection. When we do not know how to properly *react*, we usually *reject*.

Most people have the natural tendency to destroy that which they do not understand. That's why many pastors have stopped the flow of intercession in their churches. That's why they have not allowed their people to receive the ministry of deliverance. That's why we are taught that we must be overly cautious about the ministry of the prophet. And that's why many have rejected the message of the Kingdom.

We must be unconditionally willing to receive the Word of the Lord for this generation. The rejection of restorational truths in the Body of Christ must come to an end. The times demand that we be weaned from the milk of the Word. (Heb. 5:12-14.) God has "strong meat" equal to the fullness of revealed truth for this age, then our soul realm must be subjected to the higher authority of the Word of God.

I believe that if some do not stop judging the move of God, they are going to miss out totally on what God is doing in this generation. When I use the word "judge," I am not referring to discernment. I am talking about critically analyzing and intellectually rejecting the move of God.

I challenge you to allow the Holy Spirit to provide you with a new wineskin. Let us not retreat from unfamiliar surroundings in the nineties.

5

Destroying the Traditions
of the Elders

He answered and said unto them, Well hath Esaias prophesied of you hypocrites, as it is written, This people honoureth me with their lips, but their heart is far from me.

Howbeit in vain do they worship me, teaching for doctrines the commandments of men.

Making the word of God of none effect through your tradition, which ye have delivered: and many such like things do ye.

Mark 7:6,7,13

As we have noted, everything that Jesus said and did during His earthly ministry screamed of controversy and led to confrontation with the religious leaders of His day. Confronting Pharisees was a way of life to Him. Whereas most of us attempt to avoid confrontation, our Lord seemed to go out of His way to encounter it. He offended the mind in order to reveal the heart.

Challenging Man-Made Traditions

When Jesus spoke of the Pharisees' "teaching for doctrines the commandments of men" and of "making the word of God of none effect through your traditions," He was referring to the "traditions of the elders," the oral laws which had been handed down from generation to generation throughout the history of the Jewish nation. The oral laws dictated precise methods of living, and outlined specific acceptable actions outside the boundaries of the already written, established Law of God. The real conflict

Jesus encountered was the Commandments of God versus the commandments of men.

The Word of God Versus Carnal Reasonings

Even when He ministered to His own disciples, Jesus repeatedly offended their carnal reasonings. In John 6:53 our Lord made this paralyzing statement, ...**Verily, verily, I say unto you, Except ye eat the flesh of the Son of man, and drink his blood, ye have no life in you.**

Imagine what kind of effect this bold proclamation had on His disciples. Even to citizens of ancient times, this statement sounded barbaric. It smacked of cannibalism! The idea of eating the flesh and drinking the blood of man seemed grotesque to the people of Jesus' day, just as it does in our time.

Even His own disciples were weighed down with the heaviness of this statement. They complained to Him, ...**This is an hard saying; who can hear it?** (John 6:60).

The Scriptures go on to declare that **from that time many of his disciples went back, and walked no more with him** (John 6:66).

How complicated would it have been for Jesus to have explained the real meaning of His shocking words? The meaning was very simple, yet He purposely chose to keep it hidden.

For years I taught the traditional view that Jesus used parables in order to made simple the complex truths of His teachings. Then one day I discovered, to my chagrin, the real reason why parables were used. Jesus spoke parabolically not to make simple hidden truths, but to obscure simple matters:

> **And his disciples asked him, saying, What might this parable be?**
>
> **And he said, Unto you it is given to know the mysteries of the kingdom of God: but to others [I speak] in parables;**

that seeing they might not see, and hearing they might not understand.

Luke 8:9,10

Jesus purposefully made it difficult to obtain the revelation of His words. He was interested in ministering only to those who truly desired to know, for the purpose of making a total life change.

Paul the apostle stated, ...**the carnal mind is *enmity* against God: for it is not subject to the law of God, neither indeed can be** (Rom. 8:7.) The Greek word translated *enmity* in this verse also means "hatred." I have often polled Christians, asking them if they felt hatred in their carnal (natural) mind against God. The general response has been, "No! Absolutely not!" Some have even been greatly offended by my question.

You see, while we are sitting in a comfortable environment enjoying the blessings of God, our carnal mind may not oppose anything. But just let God demonstrate something new in our presence, something that may be offensive to our religious training and experience, then we will see how our natural human mind reacts. Does it become embarrassed or offended? Does it go on the defensive? Does it become angry or disturbed?

Old Testament Tests of Carnal Reasonings

Most of us in the twentieth century could not handle the Old Testament prophets like Elisha. When a group of children began to mock him and call him "baldy," he pronounced a curse on them and immediately two "she bears" came out of the woods and attacked them, severely mauling forty-two of them. (2 Kings 2:23-25.)

In another instance in which healing was called for, Elisha lay down full length upon an unconscious child, placed his mouth upon the lad's, and began to breathe the breath of life into him. (2 Kings 4:18-37.) I can just imagine the shocked reaction of certain people if some prophet of the Lord were to use that same tactic in one of our modern-day church meetings:

"That's not the way to minister healing! The proper way is to have the people line up so the prophet can lay hands on them, declaring, 'Be healed in Jesus' name!' "

Most of us could not handle Elijah any easier. While on Mount Carmel he confronted four hundred and fifty prophets of Baal, and four hundred "prophets of the groves." For the space of several hours he publicly mocked and ridiculed them. We would have a hard time accepting that kind of behavior today:

"That man is not walking in love. It's obvious that a spirit of mockery is coming forth from him."

To make matters even worse, after he had finished mocking these false prophets, he had the audacity to take a sword and kill them all — in front of witnesses! (1 Kings 18:17-40.)

Most of us could not handle Jeremiah either:

> Thus saith the Lord unto me, Go and get thee a linen girdle, and put it upon thy loins, and put it not in water.
>
> So I got a girdle according to the word of the Lord, and put it on my loins.
>
> And the word of the Lord came unto me the second time, saying,
>
> Take the girdle that thou hast got, which is upon thy loins, and arise, go to Euphrates, and hide it there in a hole of the rock.
>
> **Jeremiah 13:1-4**

Can you imagine the rumors that would circulate if it became known that our pastor had started wearing a girdle?

Of course, we recognize that this King James term refers to a wide sash or belt, as worn in the East of that day. But suppose your pastor announced to the whole city that he was wearing a sash or belt because the Lord had commanded him to do so. And then a few days later he was observed burying that same article of clothing under a large rock in the middle of an empty field. What would the community think of such actions?

Most of us could not handle Ezekiel, who was obedient to the word of the Lord which came to him, saying:

> **Lie thou also upon thy left side, and lay the iniquity of the house of Israel upon it: according to the number of the days that thou shalt lie upon it thou shalt bear their iniquity.**
>
> **For I have laid upon thee the years of their iniquity, according to the number of the days, three hundred and ninety days: so shalt thou bear the iniquity of the house of Israel.**
>
> **And when thou hast accomplished this, lie again on thy right side, and thou shalt bear the iniquity of the house of Judah forty days: I have appointed thee each day for a year.**
> **Ezekiel 4:4-6**

Can you imagine coming to church several times a week for months on end and seeing your pastor sprawled out on the sanctuary floor, lying on his left side? Consider the sheer embarrassment of it. After a while you would stop bringing visitors with you. Soon, you would even quit tithing. It wouldn't be long before whole families would be leaving the church.

Now imagine that after a year or so of this bizarre behavior on the part of your pastor, you hear that he is finally going to get up off the floor the next Sunday. Excitedly you dress the children and set off for Sunday school. In the midst of the praise and worship service, sure enough, the pastor stands to his feet. Relief floods the room.

"Perhaps he's not crazy after all," everyone sighs. "Maybe his ministry can still be salvaged — over a long period of time, of course."

But then, to everyone's surprise and dismay, he stands up just long enough to turn and lie back down on his right side.

That does it! Now you and your whole family are going to stop attending that church!

Yet that is exactly what the prophet of God was told to do. But that's not all that Ezekiel did. Let's read on to see what else the Lord commanded him:

> Take thou also unto thee wheat, and barley, and beans, and lentiles, and millet, and fitches, and put them in one vessel, and make thee bread thereof, according to the number of days that thou shalt lie upon thy side, three hundred and ninety days shalt thou eat thereof.
>
> And thou shalt eat it as barley cakes, and thou shalt bake it with dung that cometh out of man, in their sight.
>
> Then he said into me, Lo, I have given thee cow's dung for man's dung, and thou shalt prepare thy bread therewith.
>
> Ezekiel 4:9,12,15

Tell me, if you had been living in that day, do you think you would have enjoyed having Sunday dinner with Pastor Ezekiel?

The Challenge of New Anointings

Now I realize that by this time you are probably totally confused. Why would God require such bizarre, unorthodox activities on the part of His spokesmen? Is it because He wants to make His followers look ridiculous and mentally unstable? No! It's because He wants to get our attention. In every single passage that we are examining, God has a message which He wants to bring forth to His people.

This book is not a license to be "flakey" and do weird things!

That statement is so important, please allow me to repeat it:

This book is not a license to be "flakey" or do weird things!

In this book I am confronting the soul realm in order to help prepare God's people for the crucial days that lie ahead. As I have stated, there are peculiar anointings that will come on the scene, anointings that are unlike any we have ever seen before. The Church of Jesus Christ must be prepared to recognize these new and different anointings and to receive them as from the Lord.

New Testament Tests of Carnal Reasonings

Most of us couldn't handle John the Baptist. He appears on the scene, dressed in camel's hair clothes with locusts and wild honey dripping from his beard. What a picture of God's anointed spokesman!

It is painfully obvious that this poor man has a self-image problem — his diet is positively dreadful and his clothes are a disgrace! He certainly doesn't look or behave like any of the guest speakers we have had in our church lately. And he is not at all polished in his delivery. In fact, he only has one basic message: REPENT!

Many times God will require prophetic ministries to herald the same message over and over. And if you and I get tired of hearing that message, it is a positive indication that we are not walking in the revelation of it.

If we grow weary of hearing about repentance, it's because we need to repent.

If we are sick and tired of hearing about deliverance, it's because we need it.

If we are worn out with hearing about finances, that's a sure sign that we're not giving enough.

Most of us couldn't handle Jesus. I am convinced that if He walked down the aisle of most twentieth-century American churches, the ushers would be promptly ordered to remove Him from the premises.

His ministry was unconventional, to say the least. His techniques were totally inappropriate according to our sophisticated, intellectually oriented lifestyles. After all, at times He brazenly associated with sinners, dishonest tax collectors, and known prostitutes.

In His healing ministry, He rarely ever used the same method twice. In one instance He spat on the ground, made mud, and placed it upon the eyes of a blind man. (John 9:6,7.) How disgusting! Another time, He actually spat directly into a man's eyes! (Mark 8:22-25.) Could such an uncouth person truly be the Son of God?

Our Lord was never confined by convention, inhibited by prohibitions, or pressured by popular opinion. Nor did He allow Himself to be conformed to the preconceived notions of how the Son of God should look, speak and act.

Most of us couldn't even handle Agabus or any of the other New Testament prophets who came after Jesus:

> ...there came down from Judea a certain prophet, named Agabus.
>
> And when he was come unto us, he took Paul's girdle, and bound his own hands and feet, and said, Thus saith the Holy Ghost, So shall the Jews at Jerusalem bind the man that owneth this girdle, and shall deliver him into the hands of the Gentiles.
>
> **Acts 21:10,11**

How do you think you and I would react if a modern-day prophet were to come into a huge Christian convention, remove the belt and necktie from one of our most notable media ministers, tie his own hands and feet with them, and publicly predict the minister's impending imprisonment by the secular authorities?

Modern-Day Tests of Carnal Reasonings

Most of us could not handle the ministries of Rees Howell, Marie Woodworth Etter, Kathryn Kuhlman, Amy Semple McPherson, or Smith Wigglesworth.

Most Christians have a hard enough time receiving the ministries of *present-day* apostles and prophets. We feel challenged by their passion for the purposes of God.

The "traditions of the elders" have made the Word of God "of none effect" in our lives. Many of us have allowed the voice of man to influence us more than the voice of God. We have allowed the image of man to obscure the true image of Christlikeness. I challenge you to examine your life and determine whether or not you are ruled by the life-sustaining force of the Word of God, or by the death-producing "traditions of the elders."

The Call to Radical Christianity

I encourage you to lift your head high and boldly enter into the arena of the perfect will of God. Respond quickly to the clarion call to "cutting edge" Christianity. This is the hour when men and women are being required to step out of the comfort zone and live on the cutting edge. Passive Christians will be swept by the wayside as we enter into the final phase of what God is doing in relationship to planet earth.

This is not an hour for the faint-hearted or the weak-kneed. It is an hour of great destiny. The zeal of God must once again consume us. Doing the will of the Father must become our one great obsession in life. Nothing else satisfies. Nothing will fulfill our deepest internal longings quite like walking in the perfect will and ways of the Lord.

I challenge you to live radically: lay anointed hands on sick bodies, cast demons out of tormented individuals, preach the Gospel of the Kingdom with fervor and passion — and pray, pray, pray!

If you would like to receive Terry Crist's newsletter and a complete listing of all ministry materials, please write or call:

Terry Crist Ministries
P. O. Box 35889
Tulsa, OK 74153
(918) 494-0660

Books by Terry Crist

The Prophetic Church
Warring According to Prophecy
How to Move in the Miraculous
The Power of Praying in Other Tongues
Interceding Against the Powers of Darkness
The Meek Shall Inherit the Earth

Videos by Terry Crist

Rebuilding the Altars of God
Giving Birth to the Move of God
Supernatural Weapons of the Holy Spirit
Spiritual Warfare Through Intercession
The Prophetic Army

Available from your local bookstore.